joy

joy

*a godly woman's
adornment*

LYDIA BROWNBACK

::: CROSSWAY

WHEATON, ILLINOIS

Joy: A Godly Woman's Adornment

Copyright © 2010 by Lydia Brownback

Published by Crossway
        1300 Crescent Street
        Wheaton, Illinois 60187

Cover illustration: iStock

First printing 2010

Printed in the United States of America

Unless otherwise indicated, Scripture quotations are from the ESV® Bible (*The Holy Bible, English Standard Version®*), copyright © 2001 by Crossway Bibles, a publishing ministry of Good News Publishers. Used by permission. All rights reserved.

All emphases in Scripture quotations have been added by the author.

Trade paperback ISBN: 978-1-4335-1301-5

PDF ISBN: 978-1-4335-1302-2

Mobipocket ISBN: 978-1-4335-1303-9

ePub ISBN: 978-1-4335-2412-7

Library of Congress Cataloging-in-Publication Data
Brownback, Lydia, 1963–
   Joy : a godly woman's adornment / Lydia Brownback.
      p. cm. — (On-the-go devotionals)
   ISBN 978-1-4335-1301-5 (tpb)
   1. Christian women—Prayers and devotions. 2. Joy—Biblical teaching—
Meditations. 3. Suffering—Biblical teaching—Meditations. I. Title. II. Series.
BV4844.B765   2010
242'.643—dc22   2009040510

Crossway is a publishing ministry of Good News Publishers.

VP		19	18	17	16	15	14	13	12	11	10
15	14	13	12	11	10	9	8	7	6	5	4	3	2	1

With gratitude to God
for
his gift to the church
of
Cora Hogue

Contents

Introduction   9

The Devotions

Joy in Going Forward   15
Joy in Repentance   17
Joy in Rejection   20
Joy, No Matter What   22
Joy in God's Place   25
Joy in Thanksgiving   27
Joy in Letting Go   29
Joy in the Present   31
Joy in Eternity   33
Joy in Discipleship   35
Joy in Wisdom   37
Joy in Waiting   39
Good Joy and Bad Joy   42
Joy in the Path of Life   44
Persevering for Joy   46
Joy in Forgiveness   48
Joy in Being Home   51
Joy in Drawing Near to God   53
Joy in the Blessings of Others   55
The Responsibility of Joy   58
Counterfeit Joy   60
Joy in Vulnerability   62

Joy in Knowing Jesus   64
Joy in Abiding   66
Joy in Eating and Drinking   68
The Joy of Wonder   70
The Fruit of Joy   72
Joy in All God's Gifts   74
Joy in Hard Things   76
Joy in Today   78
Joy in God's Providences   81
Joy from Failure   83
Joy in God's Care   85
Joy in Prayer   87
Joy in Discernment   90
Joy in Trust   92
Joy in Full Provision   95
Joy from Rejoicing   97
Joy in Christ Alone   99
Joy in Submission   101
Joy in God's Love   103

Introduction

*J*oy. It's what makes us stand out from the world around us. Along with the gift of Christ himself comes everything we will ever really need. Our security is guaranteed. Our provision is sure. Our path is guided. Undoubtedly we pass through seasons of difficulty and sorrow and uncertainty, but real joy isn't conditioned upon our circumstances. So why are we gloomy much of the time? We don't have to be gloomy. We should most certainly not be gloomy! But all too often our thoughts and words are punctuated by grumbling and bad moods. We get caught up in looking at what we lack rather than all we have.

Most of us are privileged women, not only spiritually but temporally. That is part of our problem. We are over-privileged. Available to us is a pill for every ailment, government aid for financial difficulty, and eighteen permutations of our preferred Starbucks beverage. On top of that we have free access to the Word and the people of God. Because those things are so easily had, we have come to see our privileges as rights, but such an outlook is a joy crusher. Everything we have—health, freedom, friendship, family, job, government protection—is a gift, not a right. Remembering that, when things go wrong, keeps joy alive. Joy is always available to those indwelt by the Holy Spirit, which is why gloominess is a copout.

The apostle Paul was probably the most joyful man who ever lived, yet he had few privileges. Here is how Paul described his life:

> Far greater labors, far more imprisonments, with countless beatings, and often near death. Five times I received at the hands of the Jews the forty lashes less one. Three times I was beaten with rods. Once I was stoned. Three times I was shipwrecked; a night and a day I was adrift at sea; on frequent journeys, in danger from rivers, danger from robbers, danger from my own people, danger from Gentiles, danger in the city, danger in the wilderness, danger at sea, danger from false brothers; in toil and hardship, through many a sleepless night, in hunger and thirst, often without food, in cold and exposure. And, apart from other things, there is the daily pressure on me of my anxiety for all the churches. (2 Cor. 11:23–28)

The man who lived those things also wrote, "Rejoice in the Lord always; again I will say, Rejoice" (Phil. 4:4). Despite all he went through on a regular basis, he could rejoice because "the Lord is at hand" (v. 5). He never lost sight of who controlled his life, and he lived for his Lord: "for to me to live is Christ" (1:21). Joy and Christ-centeredness go hand-in-hand, so if we lack joy more often than we have it, might the truth be that we aren't Christ-centered? Surely, for some of us, it is. Even those of us going through a season of darkness can pursue joy, trusting that God designed us for it. Sooner or later, in Christ, we will find it. The trick for some of us is to change our self-oriented, worldly focus to Christ, and for others it is to take fresh hold of God's promises that no matter how dark life seems, he is going to push you out into the light.

First and foremost, we have to want joy. Some of us find a

perverse satisfaction in our gloom, much like a baby pitching a tantrum to get what she wants. But God doesn't respond to tantrums. Our moodiness dishonors God and robs us of the happiness that lies right at our fingertips. If we want to change—to live with perpetual joy—we must pursue it, and in Christ we are guaranteed to find it.

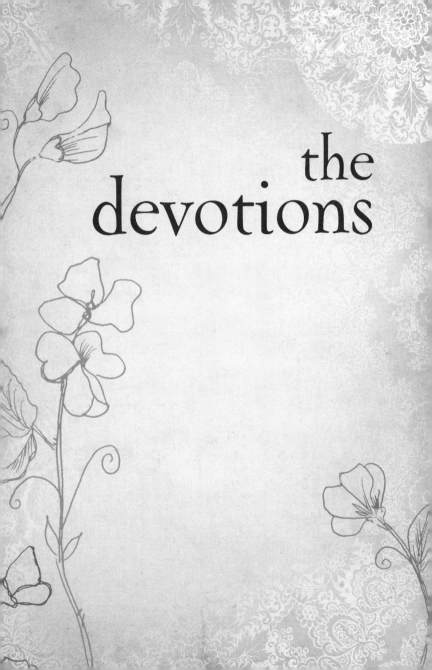

the
devotions

Joy in Going Forward

The kingdom of heaven is like treasure hidden in a field,
which a man found and covered up. Then in his joy
he goes and sells all that he has and buys that field.

MATTHEW 13:44

The man in Jesus' parable was no fence-sitter. He had found the kingdom of heaven—the rule and reign and love of God through Jesus Christ—and he was overjoyed. The wonders of it made him want more and more, and his whole life became about acquiring it. He gave all he had to get more than he could even imagine.

Such self-surrender always leads to joy. No matter what we give up for the sake of Christ and knowing God better, joy is going to result. Initially, it might not seem that way. The man in the parable had to sell all he had in order to buy the field. The time of sale is usually where we are tempted to stop. We find the kingdom of heaven, but we don't go all out to possess it fully and to let it possess us. We want Jesus but not necessarily costly discipleship. We want a kind heavenly Father, but not a disciplining one. We want our character bettered but not transformed. We want the benefits of Christianity without the cost, a price we must pay if we would go the whole way into the Christian life. Knowing this about us, Jesus said:

> Do not think that I have come to bring peace to the earth. I have
> not come to bring peace, but a sword. For I have come to set a
> man against his father, and a daughter against her mother, and
> a daughter-in-law against her mother-in-law. And a person's
> enemies will be those of his own household. Whoever loves father
> or mother more than me is not worthy of me, and whoever loves
> son or daughter more than me is not worthy of me. And who-
> ever does not take his cross and follow me is not worthy of me.
> Whoever finds his life will lose it, and whoever loses his life for
> my sake will find it. (Matt. 10:34–39)

The man in Jesus' parable did just this, and what he acquired
was far better than anything he gave up. Fence-sitters can't
know the joy of the man in the parable. Holding back is a
joy killer. Why do we cling to the possessions and desires
and personal dreams that hinder our possessing the kingdom of God more fully? Some of us do so because we aren't
convinced that what we will gain is worth whatever we will
leave behind. Others hold back because the pain of the loss
just seems too great to bear. We cannot imagine how we will
survive without that certain relationship or plan. It feels like
death. That's because it is death. It's the losing of our lives
that Jesus was talking about.

When we are facing the death of self, the costliness of discipleship, we are likely to pull back unless we remember the
promise we have been given about how it will all turn out. The
man in Jesus' parable wound up owning the field. And Jesus
said that those who lose their lives—all the earthly things they
lean on for happiness and security—will find what they have
been looking for all along. God will see to that.

Joy in Repentance

Do not be grieved,
for the joy of the LORD is your strength.

NEHEMIAH 8:10

Sin brings misery. There are no exceptions. Ever. Experience has shown us all how true this is, but we continue to sin anyway because we think that somehow, someway, this time will be different. This time we will escape. This time things will go our way. This time we will be able to manipulate the circumstances to bring us the outcome we hope for. We buy into the lie again and again, but even when we turn from God, he never turns from us. He is faithful to his unfaithful people. That's why Nehemiah, the governor of Israel, told the Israelites not to be grieved.

The hearts of the people under Nehemiah had turned away from God. The bad choices they had made over a long period had led them where sin always leads—to discouragement, loss, and feeling distant from God. (Sin never produces anything worthwhile in our lives.) But when the people heard God's Word, they were deeply convicted of sin. They were done with excuses. They had ignored the Lord and hurt him, and their awakened awareness of it brought grief to their hearts.

We grieve after we sin, too, but there is a difference between the grief of consequences suffered and that of having hurt the Lord. Only one leads to repentance. The old saying is true: being sorry for sin means being sorry enough to quit. If we are sorry primarily because our sinful choices don't work out very well, we aren't really going to quit. We will just change our tactics.

Repentance means turning around and going the other direction. It involves an active cutting off of all that has come between us and the Lord. Feelings of grief may or may not be present, but holy action will be, and as we step out in real repentance, we will find that we do feel sorry for how our sin has driven a wedge into our relationship with God. The Israelites had reached this point, and they were weeping over what their sin had done. But it was just at this point that they were surprised by joy.

Joy is the last thing we expect when the fact of our sinfulness penetrates our hearts. We know we deserve to be miserable, and so often we are tempted to wallow in misery as a way to prove how sorry we are or to try to get back in God's favor. But God doesn't want wallowing. Wallowing actually has more to do with us than with God: "Oh, Lord, *my* sin is so very bad. How could you love someone as bad as *me*?"

Instead of wallowing, godly grief embraces grace. We forget our own badness and look at God's kind heart and willingness to forgive. We look away from ourselves and toward the cross, where our badness was crucified with Christ. It is not our sin that wins the day, but God's mercy. That's why Nehemiah told the people not to be grieved. Now that they had repented and made a wholehearted commitment to turn back to the Lord, joy was theirs. They were to look away from their sin and even from their sorrow over it—away from themselves altogether—and find the joy of renewal, hope, and confident trust that would strengthen them in their way.

Are you discouraged by sin? Do you think you have forfeited joy forever because what you have done is so bad? Don't linger there. Turn back to God with all your heart, and you will find that joy is right there awaiting you.

Joy in Rejection

Then they left the presence of the council, rejoicing that they were counted worthy to suffer dishonor for the name.

Acts 5:41

"She's one of those Christians," we might overhear after rolling our grocery cart past neighborhood acquaintances in the canned goods aisle. What about us stands out as distinctly Christian so that others know it about us, even if they do not know us very well personally? It's good to be singled out as a Christian because we exude joy. It's not so good if we are the only ones on the block who darken our homes and refuse to answer the door on Halloween. Too often we get caught up in trying to *look* Christian rather than trying to *be* Christian. Even when we do stand out for reflecting Christ in a winsome way, not all our neighbors are going to like us. Some will hate us all the more, as Paul made clear: "We are the aroma of Christ to God among those who are being saved and among those who are perishing, to one a fragrance from death to death, to the other a fragrance from life to life" (2 Cor. 2:15–16).

The most joyful women I know are those most involved in serving others. No matter who likes or hates us, joy comes from living for something beyond ourselves. That's why, all through the book of Acts, we see the apostles rejoicing in the midst of horrendous difficulties. Their joy in life wasn't contingent on how well things were going personally or on how much people liked them; their whole reason for living was to spread the good news of God's love in Christ Jesus. In Acts 5 we read that they were arrested for preaching the gospel. The council decided to beat them and then let them go. Afterward, we are told, "they left the presence of the council, rejoicing that they were counted worthy to suffer dishonor for the name."

When was the last time we rejoiced at suffering dishonor for the sake of our faith? Sooner or later, we are going to be rejected for our faith by a neighbor or a family member or a friend. We might lose a job because we bear the name of Christ, or experience ridicule at work because we believe. We understand such rejection as the persecution Jesus promised all who follow him, but to rejoice at it like the apostles did? That's another story. How were they able? It wasn't because they were super-Christians. It's because they were so completely sold out to Christ that nothing mattered except him. Suffering? Great, so long as it meant they were associated with Jesus. Blessing and prosperity? Bring it on, so long as it meant God would be made more visible in their lives. God was their overarching purpose, which is why the apostles were always joyful.

The extent of joy we know is the measure of how sold out we are.

Joy, No Matter What

*I want you to know, brothers, that what has happened to me
has really served to advance the gospel.*

PHILIPPIANS 1:12

*P*aul had no idea what he was getting into when he responded
to Jesus' call on the Damascus Road. At the time of Paul's
conversion, Jesus said about him, "He is a chosen instrument
of mine to carry my name before the Gentiles and kings and
the children of Israel. For I will show him how much he must
suffer for the sake of my name" (Acts 9:15–16). Beatings,
imprisonment, hatred, and loneliness were par for the course
on Paul's missionary journeys, and eventually he suffered a
martyr's death. Yet even if Paul had known his destiny in
advance, he would have followed Jesus. That's because from
the moment he met his Savior, Jesus became his life. When
trials crashed in on him, he was not crushed, because he
viewed everything that happened to him as an instrument to
advance God's kingdom. That's why he was joyful during the
setbacks, disappointments, and difficulties.

Do we link joy and difficulty as Paul did? The joy we
find in trials most often comes after the fact. When a rough
season has passed, we are glad that God showed his faithfulness in delivering us once again, and we are joyful for

all God has taught us as a result of it, but rarely do we find ourselves joyful while still in the midst of it. We may turn to God as soon as a crisis hits, but more often than not our first cries are for relief. "Of course that's what we do! It's only human," you might be saying. It is human, and besides that, God wants us to pray for relief. Surely Paul prayed for relief from his troubles too, but relief wasn't his primary concern. First and foremost in his heart was the advance of God's kingdom. That is why he was joyful. He had no idea if his circumstances would work out so that his life could flow along comfortably, but he knew that God's kingdom would advance through the outcome, whatever it was.

The reason we lack joy in our trials is that we are set on an outcome that will make our lives easier. What does Paul's outlook reveal about God? If Paul suffered so much yet retained his joy, it tells us more about God than about Paul. It reveals that following God, no matter the cost, must be worth it.

Also, when we cling to Christ in faith during hard times, others notice. It's easy to express our trust in God's love when all is going smoothly, but he is doubly glorified when we express it during seasons of pain. We might agree with all this in theory, but when the chips are down, in the midst of perplexing difficulties, we are more often characterized by fear and doubt than by trust and joy. But our moments of doubt and discouragement do not cancel out God's power; he is much bigger than that. It isn't human to rejoice in suffering; it is supernatural. God is glorified not by calling strong women but by giving his strength to weak women.

Maybe you are suffering right now, and you are tempted to wonder why God doesn't deliver you sooner from your painful or perplexing situation. One reason is that God has promised to use our suffering to give us a greater capacity for joy. Paul's suffering, although extremely painful, didn't bring him down for long, because he wasn't concerned for himself. How joyful we could be in times of trouble if our primary focus, our top priority, is what God is doing through it—for us, for others, and for his glory.

If we are in the midst of a difficult season, are we willing to rejoice and to view it as an opportunity to see more of God's power and goodness? Being called to suffer is actually a privilege. Each trial is a gift. It's a chance to know God's strength and supernatural joy and to show that following him is worth everything.

Joy in God's Place

For all the gods of the peoples are idols,
but the LORD made the heavens.
Splendor and majesty are before him;
strength and joy are in his place.

1 CHRONICLES 16:26-27

*W*e always—every moment, without exception—pursue what we believe will make us happy. For some it's a particular relationship. For others it's a certain home. For still others it's a career path. Whatever it is, we devote ourselves to getting it, pursuing it with all our energy and every resource we have. We are certainly free to delight in the material and relational blessings God brings us, but if we believe our happiness is dependent on them, it's because, whether we realize it or not, we don't really believe God is enough for us.

We say that God is enough, but the fact that we hover and worry and fret when our goals and hopes don't pan out proves otherwise. Jesus said, "Where your treasure is, there your heart will be also" (Matt. 6:21). How do we respond when something we value is taken away? Do we cling to Christ in our sorrow or disappointment, or do we resist him and set ourselves on a determined course to prevent the loss or recapture it? Our attitude toward God in life's ups and downs is always the most honest depiction of what we really believe.

We will never ultimately find the happiness we seek in anything this world offers—even the good things—because we have been wired to find it in God alone. Joy is found only in God's "place," wherever and however he leads us deeper into his fellowship. Joy—biblical joy—is one way for us to know if we are dwelling in God's place. Godly joy springs from living in harmony with God, having a mind set on pleasing him. If that underlies our pursuits, we are in God's place.

If we insist on defining and establishing our own place, we won't find joy, nor will we ever get to where we think we want to go. James Boice wrote:

> If you think you are going to get rich through a job that excludes God and a Christian witness, God will let you get close enough to the wealth to taste it but then keep it just beyond your grasp. If you think you are going to become famous in show business and are willing to leave the commands of God behind in your upward scramble to get there, God will let you get close enough to know and envy others who have made it but keep you an unknown. Do you think that God will not do this: That He is too "kind"? I tell you that God will do it. He is faithful to His nature and will not allow the one He loves to be destroyed through an adulterous infatuation with this world's idols.[1]

God's place is first place, whether it be in our relationships, our homes, or our jobs, and he will reign there only if he reigns supreme in our hearts.

Concerning all the varied details of your life, are you dwelling in God's place or your own? Joy, or lack thereof, is a way to know. Joy is always present where God reigns supreme.

---

[1] James Boice, *Minor Prophets* (Grand Rapids, MI: Kregel, 1986), 25.

Joy in Thanksgiving

Do all things without grumbling or questioning.

PHILIPPIANS 2:14

*P*aul's command might not seem too difficult until we consider what "all things" actually entails. Have you grumbled about the weather lately? How about a sore throat? We might feel convicted when we grumble about the little daily inconveniences, but we feel justified in complaining when the major crises hit. What else can we do when our husband loses his job or we get the news that our child has serious learning disabilities? But Paul meant what he said. "All things" means all things, because there is nothing—absolutely nothing—that touches our lives that somehow slipped through the cracks of his providential ordering.

When we grumble about the weather, we are arguing against God's ordering of creation. When we complain about illness or job loss or whatever it may be, we are declaring, whether we realize it or not, that God isn't handling our affairs very well. Complaining is actually a form of pride, which makes sense when we recognize its rebellious undertones.

There just isn't any need to complain, because whatever circumstances God sends—rain and snow, sickness, and trouble of various kinds—he sends in order to bless us. But it is impossible to keep an eye out for God's blessings while harboring a complaining spirit. Grumbling about hard things blocks our expectation of good things, and if we are not looking for the good things, we may fail to see them when they come. That's part of why thankfulness is so important. Offering thanks to God, no matter what is going on in our lives, is a way of acknowledging that he knows exactly what he is doing and that we can trust him.

The antidote to a complaining spirit is a thankful spirit. "Give thanks in all circumstances," Paul wrote, "for this is the will of God in Christ Jesus for you" (1 Thess. 5:18). Sometimes thankfulness is a choice we make rather than a feeling we have. We can choose to give thanks even when we don't feel like it. God is pleased when he sees our willingness to give thanks because it demonstrates our trust in his goodness and our willingness to let him run the show. If we practice thanksgiving, before we know it we will actually find ourselves feeling thankful, which is always accompanied by joy. God delights to bless a thankful heart.

Joy in Letting Go

Indeed, I count everything as loss because of the
surpassing worth of knowing Christ Jesus my Lord.
For his sake I have suffered the loss of all things and
count them as rubbish, in order that I may gain Christ
and be found in him, not having a righteousness of my own
that comes from the law, but that which comes through
faith in Christ, the righteousness from God
that depends on faith.

PHILIPPIANS 3:8–9

*N*othing measures up to knowing and living with Jesus. Do
we really believe that? We must, because it is what we were
created for. That's why nothing else brings lasting satisfaction
and joy. If we trust God's Word, we know the truth of this.
Why, then, do we strive so hard to find fulfillment elsewhere?
It never works—certainly not in any lasting way. Paul knew
the secret to possessing and enjoying the blessings of earthly
life is to hold them loosely. Paul held all his blessings loosely
because he had found something that mattered even more. He
had found life in Christ to surpass the best that this life
can offer. That's why he sought to get rid of anything that
would hinder or water down a deeper intimacy with his Lord.

The value we place on Christ can be measured by what we are willing to forego or give up in order to safeguard our relationship with him. It can also be measured by how we react when God takes away something we value. Do we get angry with God? Do we get depressed about it? He removes from us only what he knows will impede our spiritual growth. If we fight against his providences, inwardly or outwardly, it is an indicator that Christ is not our all. If he were, we would be eager to hunt down and set aside any interference.

Paul gave up prestige, power, authority, friends, the comforts of prosperity, and eventually his very own life. Is there something in our lives that we know is a spiritual hindrance but have been unwilling to lose for the surpassing worth of knowing Christ better? For some, it might be a relationship. For others, it might be a particular calling, or a home, or an education. For still others, it might be good health. Whatever it is, letting go of it will lead to joy.

Many of us are familiar with the now-famous words penned by missionary Jim Elliot months before he was martyred for his faith: "He is no fool who gives what he cannot keep to gain what he cannot lose." Jim knew what Paul did and what we can too—those who leave precious things to follow Christ have no regrets.

Joy in the Present

Brothers, I do not consider that I have made it my own.
But one thing I do: forgetting what lies behind and
straining forward to what lies ahead,
I press on toward the goal for the prize of the upward call
of God in Christ Jesus.

PHILIPPIANS 3:13-14

*G*ood or bad, the past can undo us. Bad memories can act like quicksand on our state of mind, sucking us down into a vortex of misery. Memories of sin are hard to forget if its consequences have followed us into the present. Regret over broken relationships or bad choices can hound us for years afterward. But good memories can be equally destructive to present joy. When we dwell fondly on a particular time in the past, we tend to forget the not-so-good aspects of that past season. Nostalgia is deceitful, as Sarah Groves sings:

> *I've been painting pictures of Egypt, leaving out what it lacked.*
> *The future feels so hard, and I want to go back.*

But her song doesn't end there:

> *The places I used to turn to can't hold the things I've learned,*
> *and that road was closed off to me while my back was turned.*[1]

---
[1]Sarah Groves, "Painting Pictures of Egypt," *Conversations*, Sponge Records, 2000.

Paul made a choice to close off the road to his past. He found real life in the present and even more so in the goal out in front of him—the upward call of God in Christ. Paul simply chose to forget all about the past and, for him, that was no small task. He'd lost much in order to live for Christ. If we belong to Christ, what we are heading toward is far superior to anything we leave behind. Solomon wrote, "Say not, 'Why were the former days better than these?' for it is not from wisdom that you ask this" (Eccl. 7:10). Are you holding on to something from your past? Do you spend excessive time and energy trying to capture the good old days? If so, you are going to find little joy in the present. We can cultivate a willingness to let go of the past by setting our minds on all we have in Christ both now and forever.

Joy in Eternity

Our citizenship is in heaven, and from it we await a Savior,
the Lord Jesus Christ, who will transform our lowly body
to be like his glorious body, by the power that
enables him even to subject all things to himself.

PHILIPPIANS 3:20-21

We all belong by birth or vocation to a particular country, and due to our citizenship our government has claims on us. We must obey laws and pay taxes. But wherever we live, our primary citizenship is nowhere on earth. If we belong to Christ, our primary country is the kingdom of God, and it is in that kingdom that happiness is to be found.

No small portion of Paul's joy came from his awareness of his true country, his permanent home. He lived for the day when his spiritual citizenship would become the real thing. He lived in expectation of seeing Jesus face-to-face. He waited eagerly for his final transformation into Christlikeness, and he was sure it would happen because he trusted God's promises.

We are citizens of the same heavenly country, but often it fails to bring us the joy that it brought to Paul. We tend not to be heavenly minded. We aren't focused eagerly on the return of Jesus Christ but on our families, jobs, time, money, and overall well-being today. We live to mold our lives around what makes us happy today. We struggle to admit it, but heaven just seems so far away and unreal. Today is what we have to deal with; we will think about the return of Jesus and the life to come at a more convenient time. But Paul had just as many daily cares as we do. It seems clear, then, that he made a choice of where to place his hope, and it wasn't on working out the earthly details to his best advantage.

We have the same choice on the same daily basis. Paul's mindset was a choice, and what he chose to focus on fueled his joy. We tend to be pragmatic women—if it works, we try it. We are always looking for what works. Not Paul. He looked at what God had already worked for him—his salvation in Christ—and for all it would mean to him for eternity. Paul was no Pollyanna, looking for an optimistic twist to every difficulty. He was looking at his reality, which was his real home in a permanent kingdom. That is our home, too, if we belong to Christ. Compared to eternity, our life on earth is shorter than the blink of an eye, yet we are so consumed by what occurs in that one quick blink. Paul understood this, which is why his focus on the next life was no mere avoidance technique. It was his reality. It is ours too.

Joy in Discipleship

*I rejoiced in the Lord greatly that now at length
you have revived your concern for me. You were indeed
concerned for me, but you had no opportunity.
Not that I am speaking of being in need,
for I have learned in whatever situation I am to be content.*

PHILIPPIANS 4:10–11

Advertisements tell us, "Have it your way"; and, "Though some things in life are priceless, for everything else there's MasterCard." Personal and immediate gratification is the name of the American game, which is perhaps why it's so hard for those of us born and raised in America to experience the sort of contentment that characterized Paul. We find contentment when everything is going well, but for many of us it's a completely different ballgame during times of trouble. Advertising fuels our struggle because it bombards us with all the things we absolutely "must have" in order to be happy. We're told that without a particular house or car or hair color or spouse, we are doomed to unhappiness.

Paul was not naïve about the pleasures that accompany material prosperity. He was no stranger to the finer things of life. Paul had grown up in better circumstances than many men of his day in terms of social class and education, but his new life as an itinerant preacher and missionary required him to leave behind most of his former privileges. Yet he was still content; in fact, he was more content than previously, when he'd had it all by worldly standards.

True discipleship will always, at some point or another, require us to forego one or more advantages that the world offers. When that happens, we are going to respond in one of three ways. We will let it go and count it well lost, as Paul did. Or we will try to hang on to whatever it is we are being called to forego and seek to somehow fit it into our life of faith. Or we will walk away from following Christ altogether. Only one of those options will enable joy, and we know it, so why do we hesitate? Why do we cling so tightly to anything that hinders our walk with God? J. I. Packer exposes what underlies our unwillingness:

> We shrink from breaking with social conventions in order to serve Christ because we fear that if we did, the established structure of our life would collapse all around us, leaving us without a footing anywhere. It is these half-conscious fears, this dread of insecurity, rather than any deliberate refusal to face the cost of following Christ, which make us hold back. We feel that the risks of out-and-out discipleship are too great for us to take. In other words, we are not persuaded of the adequacy of God to provide for all the needs of those who launch out wholeheartedly on the deep sea of unconventional living in obedience to the call of Christ. . . . We are afraid to go all the way in accepting the *authority* of God, because of our secret *uncertainty* as to his adequacy to look after us if we do. . . . There is no ultimate loss or irreparable impoverishment to be feared; if God denies us something, it is only in order to make room for one or other of the things he has in mind.[1]

Are we willing? Joy is possible no other way.

---

[1] J. I. Packer, *Knowing God* (Downers Grove, IL: InterVarsity Press, 1973), 246.

Joy in Wisdom

Folly is a joy to him who lacks sense,
but a man of understanding walks straight ahead.

PROVERBS 15:21

There is good joy and bad joy, and sometimes it is hard to discern the difference. Another Proverb puts it like this: "There is a way that seems right to a man, but its end is the way to death" (14:12). We are in constant danger of confusing what's right with what feels good. The Word of God is the only way to know for sure.

"But the Bible doesn't speak to my situation," you might be thinking. However, the Bible does speak to your situation and to everyone's, at all times. If we believe it does not, it is likely because we are looking there only for black-and-white answers. There are plenty of those in Scripture. We find an unequivocal no to questions about marrying an unbeliever or abusing alcohol, for example. Answers to everything else come from immersing ourselves in the Word as a whole. As we do, we discover that it increasingly shapes our thinking about what to do in every situation. Rather than black-and-white answers, we begin to look for wisdom. What God would have us do in a given situation becomes increasingly straightforward the more we know him, and the way we know him is through the Word. Immersing ourselves in the Word is to immerse ourselves in the character of God.

Sometimes, despite regular attendance on the Word of God and prayer, we still aren't sure what to do. Could it be that we really don't want to know? Maybe we are finding significant joy in something—a friendship, a pursuit, a pastime—and we sense that if we look too closely, we might find that God's glory and our walk with him is diminished because of it. At some level, we know it isn't God's best. "Whoever knows the right thing to do and does not do it, to him it is sin" (James 4:17). A real test is whether we are heeding wise council or arguing against it. It is almost sure that if we spurn the wisdom of godly people and go after what we want, it will not end well.

Wisdom is recognizing worldly joy as folly, turning from it, and walking straight ahead. We cannot go wrong if we do that. No matter what we leave behind, we will find real joy only in paths of wisdom.

Joy in Waiting

Though the fig tree should not blossom,
nor fruit be on the vines,
the produce of the olive fail
and the fields yield no food,
the flock be cut off from the fold
and there be no herd in the stalls,
yet I will rejoice in the Lord;
I will take joy in the God of my salvation.

HABAKKUK 3:17-18

Habakkuk the prophet didn't understand why God didn't seem to be answering his prayers. "How long shall I cry for help, and you will not hear?" he cries to God (Hab. 1:2). Evil was flourishing in Habakkuk's day, God's people were suffering because of it, and God didn't seem to be doing anything about it.

We can all relate to Habakkuk. Things go wrong and we plead with God to intervene, yet things don't change. Laws pass enabling abortion to be easier to get at a later trimester. A school teacher gets fired because she erects a manger scene in her classroom at Christmastime. A doctor contracts HIV as the result of treating an AIDS-infected accident victim. A mother-to-be gets the news that there is no heartbeat three days before the delivery date. The stories are endless. We've heard them; we've lived our own. Where is God in all these things?

We will never know lasting joy in the Lord if we seek to understand him by what goes on in the world or by our circumstances. The only way to joy is to interpret our circumstances by God's Word rather than to judge God by our circumstances. God's ways often don't make sense to us. He doesn't act the way we think a sovereign, loving Father should act, and we find ourselves questioning his goodness or his power or his involvement in our lives. We don't see that our understanding of everything is so very small whereas God's understanding is infinite. It is impossible for us to see that everything going on in the world and in every life at every moment is being directed by God for the good of his people and the praise of his glory.

Someday we will see that, but for now, joy comes when we trust as Habakkuk did. Rather than judging God by what he could see, Habakkuk sought the Lord, and the Lord answered him:

> For still the vision awaits its appointed time;
>   it hastens to the end—it will not lie.
> If it seems slow, wait for it;
>   it will surely come; it will not delay. (Hab. 2:3)

Habakkuk was given a prophetic word that everything would work out all right for God's people. He had only to trust that word and then wait for God's timing. Habakkuk took the long view because he trusted God, and he wound up joyful.

We can do likewise because we, too, have God's Word,

which promises "that for those who love God all things work together for good" (Rom. 8:28). When it is God's time to act—whether globally or in our individual lives—nothing will stand in the way. In the meantime, no matter how grim things might seem, we can be filled with joy because God is faithful to his promises. He will surely come.

Good Joy and Bad Joy

Haman went out that day joyful and glad of heart.
But when Haman saw Mordecai in the king's gate,
that he neither rose nor trembled before him, he was filled
with wrath against Mordecai.

ESTHER 5:9

*N*ot all joy springs from Christ. There is a joy that comes from selfish gratification, and that is the sort that Haman had. Haman was an enemy of the Jews, God's people, and he posed a great threat to them due to his high position in the court of the Persian king Ahasuerus, the ruling power of the ancient world at the time.

Haman was joyful and glad of heart because things were going his way. Queen Esther had just issued her request that Haman and the king attend a feast that she would prepare for them. Dinner with the king and queen! Haman had finally "arrived." His power was growing, and he felt good about life and about himself. He could throw his weight around and do as he wished with the Jews.

We condemn Haman, but how much of the joy we experience comes from selfish gain? Our Bible knowledge is more extensive than that of others in the Bible study. Our efforts at the gym have paid off—we look better than others at the party. We get the man that other girls like. Detecting selfish joy in our hearts can be difficult because we are blind to much of our sinfulness, but one way that we can detect selfish joy is by its fleeting nature. Haman's joy dissipated the moment he left the king's gate and came across the Jew Mordecai. Mordecai wasn't fooled by Haman, nor was he intimidated by him, so Mordecai showed Haman no respect. He refused to bow and scrape before Haman or to be afraid of his power. In an instant Haman's well-being was wiped out and replaced by rage. Joy can be sustained only as long as its source remains constant, and since the source of Haman's joy—his personal greatness— was threatened by Mordecai, it evaporated.

The same thing happens to us. Selfish joy is utterly dependent on things continuing to go our way, so when something upsets the applecart on which our joy is relying, we too are plunged into anger or anxiety or depression. Joy is the outworking of worship. If we worship ourselves or a relationship or a job or a house or physical fitness, we will wind up doing what Haman did next. Haman felt he could not go on until he had dealt with Mordecai, crushing the man who threatened his sinful happiness. So he set about manipulating circumstances to regain his sense of well-being. Things didn't go well for Haman. He lost his position and his power and, indeed, his very life.

That is always the result of self-worship and of setting our hearts on bettering our lives through the things of this world. True joy, lasting joy, comes only from worshiping a sure thing—Jesus Christ. Are we finding that joy is fleeting, here one day and gone the next? Are we easily angered when things don't go our way or when we lose something we've worked hard for or when someone else gets what we wanted? If so, it is likely that the joy we felt was not the Spirit-given joy that God has designed us for. His joy is the only kind that lasts.

Joy in the Path of Life

You make known to me the path of life;
in your presence there is fullness of joy;
at your right hand are pleasures forevermore.

PSALM 16:11

*D*eep, abiding, constant joy—fullness of joy—is found only in God's presence. That is why there is a direct correlation between the joy we experience and our walk with God. Certainly troubles come in and disrupt our feelings of joy and make God seem distant, and there are occasions of God's parental discipline that seem anything but joyful. "For the moment all discipline seems painful rather than pleasant" (Heb. 12:11). But the fact remains that dwelling closely with God produces joy.

It is only in close fellowship with God that we come to know what he is really like. We can read good Christian books, sign up for gospel conferences where the Word is taught, and spend the majority of our time with other believers, but Christian activities alone won't bring us the fullness of joy that the psalmist is describing here. Joy will ripen only as Christian activities drive us closer to God himself. He is a relational God, and he designed us to fellowship with him intimately. Those who radiate the greatest joy are the ones who relate most personally to God.

As a result of his intensely personal relationship with God, the psalmist, David, had come to understand God's dealings with him in day-to-day life. He had learned that all the good in his life had come directly from God's hand (Ps. 16:2). He knew that God had ordered every aspect of his life, and therefore he was able to say, "The lines have fallen for me in pleasant places; indeed, I have a beautiful inheritance" (v. 6). He had experienced the Lord's counsel in varied circumstances (v. 7). David was peaceful in the ups and downs of life (v. 8). These are the fruits of a life lived in close fellowship with God, something he desires for each one of us.

How do we get there? We do what David did: "I have set the LORD always before me" (v. 8). There are plenty of seminars and books on the importance of cultivating a good marriage, but our relationship with God is even more important. We don't need ten tips to a better spiritual life. What we need is to put God out front in our thoughts, priorities, time, and activities. If we allow his Word to govern us, we will see that he delights to show us "the path of life" and the path for our life. We will find pleasures forevermore and understand what David meant by "fullness of joy."

Persevering for Joy

For his anger is but for a moment,
and his favor is for a lifetime.
Weeping may tarry for the night,
but joy comes with the morning.

PSALM 30:5

Sometimes joy is hard won. We have to fight for it.[1] But when the battle is especially strong, we get tempted to give up the fight and settle for so much less. If only we would keep the end—joy—in view! Living as we do in a culture marked by impatience and quick gratification, we have come to see perseverance as a virtue obtainable by only a select few, so it is no wonder we give up. Rather than wrestle with God through difficult and downcast seasons, we take a pill. Rather than acknowledge the sin that underlies so much of our relational dysfunction, we blame the upbringing we had. Is it any wonder that we don't know lasting joy?

We tolerate sin and its effects every day—our own and that of others—and it displeases God greatly, but his displeasure is never the end of the story for God's children. Unlike human parents, God never disciplines in anger. His goal is

---

[1] A good book on fighting for joy is John Piper's *When I Don't Desire God: How to Fight for Joy* (Wheaton, IL: Crossway, 2004).

always corrective and redemptive, never punitive. Christ bore God's anger for every sin the Christian has ever or will ever commit. Therefore, "it is for discipline that you have to endure. God is treating you as sons. For what son is there whom his father does not discipline? . . . For the moment all discipline seems painful rather than pleasant, but later it yields the peaceful fruit of righteousness to those who have been trained by it" (Heb. 12:7, 11).The consequences for sin are painful and sometimes long-lasting, perhaps for a lifetime. God could put a stop to them—and sometimes he does. But often he lets them linger, and when he does, he is disciplining—training, not punishing—us. Such discipline is part and parcel of his favor toward us, which will never cease.

Much of our sorrows in life come about not so much from our personal sin as from the sin of the entire fallen world. All our suffering is somehow the result of sin, even when it's not our own. So will we give up? Will we turn away from hope when the going gets too painful and opt instead for the short-term, shallow joys of this life? They are available in abundance, so it is easy to do, and many of us choose that path and miss out on the abundant joy God wants for us in Christ.

Your quick fix might be different from mine, but we've all got one ready at hand. For some, a quick fix is as close as the refrigerator or the Internet. For others, it's a job change or a move to another part of the country. Whatever it might be, recognize it for what it is. Weeping may—and will—endure for a night. But for those who trust in the Lord, joy will inevitably come in the morning, and the morning may be a lot closer than we think.

Joy in Forgiveness

Let me hear joy and gladness;
let the bones that you have broken rejoice.
Hide your face from my sins,
and blot out all my iniquities.

P S A L M   5 1 : 8 – 9

*N*o true child of God can be happy in a backslidden state, and what a mercy that is! When we get off on a sinful path, God presses down upon us, seeking to woo us back to himself. One of the first things he is likely to press away is our joy. Even though he is offended and hurt by our turning away toward sin, he doesn't let us go. His love is the sort that pursues those who run from him. But if we keep on running, his pursuit is going to get painful. There will come a time when God will turn us over to our sin. He abandons us to our willfulness, not because he gets tired of us or gives up on us, but to bring us to repentance. James Boice occasionally pointed out in his sermons that if we are true Christians, we cannot ever sin so badly that we are in danger of losing our salvation because God will do one of two things: either he will make us so miserable that we beg him to get us out of it, or he will take our life away. Either way, we are under the care of our Shepherd, who will not let us go.

joy

We do not have to let our sin get so extreme that extreme measures are required to bring us back. We can avoid unnecessary grief by heeding the voice of our conscience and that Spirit-given weight of sin's conviction before we silence them, something we will do if we continue on a sinful path. The psalmist describes it well:

> When I kept silent, my bones wasted away
>   through my groaning all day long.
> For day and night your hand was heavy upon me;
>   my strength was dried up as by the heat of summer.
>
> I acknowledged my sin to you,
>   and I did not cover my iniquity;
> I said, "I will confess my transgressions to the LORD,"
>   and you forgave the iniquity of my sin. (Ps. 32:3–5)

The psalmist heeded that pressing weight. King David, who penned both Psalm 32 and 51, understood that the conviction of sin is a mercy, and he repented. If we ignore it, eventually our conscience gets seared and the Spirit-given alarm bells grow faint and distant. Before long, our sin doesn't seem so bad to us, and we start wondering why we ever thought it was wrong. That is a dangerous place to be, because it means we are beginning to experience God's judgment. He is turning us over to what we think we want so badly in order to show us that we really don't want it after all.

David's cries of confession were accompanied by cries of sorrow for his sin and a turning back to the Lord. He wanted his joy back, and once he repented, he felt freedom to ask for new joy. Are you weighted down by the knowledge of some sin in your life that you have been refusing to deal with? If so, I can say with confidence that you are not happy. In fact, if you slow down and really take a look, you will see that you are miserable. Don't wait. Go back to the God who is waiting for you, and once you have, ask him to renew your joy.

Joy in Being Home

My soul longs, yes, faints
for the courts of the LORD;
my heart and flesh sing for joy
to the living God.

PSALM 84:2

Those who know the greatest joy are those who yearn for God's presence and pursue it, and they yearn for it because they have tasted how good it is. Can we relate to the psalmist's words? Do we know this yearning? If not, it's because there is competition. Rather than yearning for God, we yearn for a manageable life, and eventually we don't yearn for him nearly so much as we yearn for that husband or baby or house or promotion. We pour so much of our energies into obtaining lesser joys that we lose our taste for the real one. C. S. Lewis called it playing in mud puddles when we could be vacationing at the beach.

The only way our heart and flesh will sing for joy as the psalmist's did is if we make our home with God. What is home? Home is where we let our guard down. It's where we are free to say what's on our mind and be ourselves. We don't have to wear makeup or use the proper fork. We can simply live in freedom, trusting that those who live with us want us there just as we are. That's the kind of relationship the psalmist knew with God, and it's what we are called to also. We can let our guard down with God because Jesus Christ covers us in his presence. Sinful though we are, in Christ we have absolute freedom to be ourselves with God.

God was the psalmist's home, which in his day was housed in the temple in Jerusalem. He wrote this psalm in anticipation of being welcomed into the temple, into God's presence, after journeying to get there. Today that temple where God is housed lies within each one of us in Christ. God dwells within us through Christ by means of the Holy Spirit. We do not need to make a long pilgrimage to get to God's house, as the psalmist did. He yearned to get there. We have already arrived. But instead of basking in all that's there for us, we look outside for other pleasures. Those who reached the ancient temple cried, "How lovely is your dwelling place, O LORD of hosts!" (v. 1) and "Blessed are those who dwell in your house, ever singing your praise!" (v. 4). They didn't look out the temple windows for something better. They knew they'd found what their souls longed for.

Are we seeking or settling for what lies outside that window onto the world? We've got all we need in Christ. If we look at him, we will know exactly what the psalmist meant when he said, "A day in your courts is better than a thousand elsewhere. I would rather be a doorkeeper in the house of my God than dwell in the tents of wickedness" (v. 10).

Joy in Drawing Near to God

Light is sown for the righteous,
and joy for the upright in heart.

PSALM 97:11

*T*here is a direct link between joy and heartfelt obedience. We may find a measure of satisfaction in outward conformity, but never joy. That is why the psalmist claims joy as a blessing for the upright *in heart.*

Simply going through the Christian motions works for a time, but in the long run it leads only to weariness, discouragement, and, if we aren't careful, disillusionment or falling into sin. So often we kid ourselves about where we are spiritually. We are doing the right things, attending the right functions, and raising our kids with right morals, but there is no vitality in our walk with God. How can we tell? Absence of joy might be a clue.

Busy mothers of young children have perhaps the hardest time maintaining a vital, joy-filled faith. Exhaustion, lack of adult companionship, and the endless routine of mundane tasks leave little time to sneak off alone for Bible reading and prayer. How do we break out of this? I know one mother who gets up in the middle of the night to meet with God for an hour (the only time when the house is quiet), and the practice has revitalized her. God has blessed her efforts to seek him:

she actually finds she has more energy for the routine rather than less, despite the added loss of sleep. This won't work for every mother, however. I know many who have tried.

Mothers or not, we all go through seasons in which our faith walk seems to be in mere maintenance mode rather then thriving and vital. It is a testing of our faith. At such times we find out whether our faith rests on the truth of Christ or on the good feelings we get after a lengthy quiet time. Although time alone with God in the word is vital, ultimately, being upright in heart means simply relying on Christ, and so long as we are doing that, we are growing spiritually.

Sometimes, however, we settle for going through the motions or even simply choose to do so. We make ourselves too busy to get alone with God. Perhaps we are avoiding something we know he wants us to deal with. Maybe we have doubts lurking in our hearts about God, and we are afraid of what will happen if we look too closely at them. At such times, we are prone to settle for outward obedience and convince ourselves that our hearts are right with God. But if joy is persistently absent, something isn't working as it should.

Are you living in spiritual maintenance mode? If so, perhaps there is little else you can do at the moment due to life's circumstances, but there is still cause for rejoicing because it is an opportunity to rely more fully on Christ rather than on your spiritual efforts. If you will do so, you are likely to find joy returning long before your circumstances change. If, however, "maintenance mode" is your choice, you are, along with that choice, choosing to remain joyless. Is perhaps the absence of joy a call from God, sent to get your attention and draw you near?

Joy in the Blessings of Others

*The heart knows its own bitterness,
and no stranger shares its joy.*

Proverbs 14:10

No matter how many comforters one has, grieving is the loneliest activity on earth. We may be surrounded by friends when a loved one leaves us, but we still feel utterly alone. In one way, we are. Our friends can offer hugs and words of comfort, but they can't get inside our skin and know what we are feeling. Human sympathy may abound, but human empathy isn't fully possible. No one can completely grasp what another experiences during a particular loss—the memories and history that accompany it, the words left unsaid, the inevitable regrets.

The same is true of our happinesses, which, while certainly easier to bear than sorrows, are experienced in some measure in isolation. In some ways happiness may be even lonelier than sorrow, because there are always going to be those who can't or won't rejoice with us. A woman becomes engaged to be married, and her single friends are too anxious about their own single state to rejoice with her, and although they won't admit it, they are just a bit too jealous to be genuinely glad for their friend. Our obtainment of a husband, a house, or a baby—earthly joys desired by most women—so easily evokes the envy of others, dimming our delight in our blessing. We feel the need to harness our happiness around those those who perceive themselves to be less fortunate.

Proverbs 14:10 tells us that, in the long run, as far as people go, we are really on our own. God is the only one who knows exactly what we feel and why we feel it. Jesus experienced the same joys and pains that we do—real empathy—and he alone has the power to minister to us in exactly the way we need and to bring balm to our loneliness. "We do not have a high priest who is unable to sympathize with our weaknesses, but one who in every respect has been tempted *as we are*, yet without sin. Let us then with confidence draw near to the throne of grace that we may receive mercy and find grace to help in time of need" (Heb. 4:15–16).

God's character is relational, and because of that he rejoices when we rejoice and grieves when we sorrow. Consider how sad Jesus was at the death of Lazarus, when his sisters were overcome with grief. John tells us that Jesus wept (see John 11). Since empathy and sympathy are inherent to God's character, he calls us to embrace what others are going through. "Rejoice with those who rejoice, weep with those who weep," Paul wrote (Rom. 12:15). While the fact remains that ultimately we rejoice and sorrow independently, we reflect God's character when we grieve at others' losses and take pleasure in their blessings.

Years ago I worked in an office with three young women, all of whom were engaged and planning to be married in short time. I was struggling with being single then, but I pasted a smile on my face every day as I listened to the latest updates about dresses and invitations and gift registries.

Underneath the smiles, however, I wasn't happy for my colleagues. They were all younger than I; it seemed quite unfair that they were getting married, when I wasn't.

One day that summer I went into my office and closed the door and asked God to work real happiness in my heart for my younger engaged colleagues. And he did. In fact, from that moment on, I never felt anything but joy at the news of another's engagement or wedding. A supernatural work? Yes, absolutely. And the speed and the extent at which God answered my prayer showed me that our rejoicing with others matters to God. God is surely willing to do the same in all our hearts, whatever the sticking point may be.

The real question then isn't whether God will do it, but whether we are willing for him to do it. Are we willing to rejoice with others, even when we go without whatever it is God is giving to them? If so, we will actually participate in the joy of others' blessings in no small measure.

The Responsibility of Joy

A joyful heart is good medicine,
but a crushed spirit dries up the bones.

PROVERBS 17:22

*G*od created us for joy, so when joy is absent for long seasons there are bound to be physical effects. A joyless woman is living counter to her design. That's why we need to cultivate joy the same we way take care to get enough sleep and to eat right. To cultivate joy is to practice good stewardship, not only of our spirit but also of our body.

How do we cultivate joy? We find it elusive sometimes simply because we live in a fallen world, and we are touched by the effects of sin everywhere we turn. Times of grief and loss come to all of us and can banish joy for a season, but if we cling to God while we grieve, we will be driven closer to him in the process, and joy will overtake us once again, even as we continue to sorrow. Grieving that refuses solace and wallows in misery is really a refusal to accept a loss that God has allowed. Self-pity is the sister of pride, and so long as we linger in it, joy won't even be on our horizon.

Too, unrepentant sin is always a hindrance to joy. If we have negotiated a truce with some known sin, we can be sure that what joy we have is not Spirit-given. We all fear sin's consequences, but one we often don't consider is the loss of Spirit-given joy. It is this joy that comprises the good medicine held forth in Proverbs. Elisabeth Elliot wrote, "Much sickness—physical, mental, and emotional—surely must come from disobedience. When the soul is confronted with an alternative of right or wrong and chooses to blur the distinction, making excuses for its bewilderment and frustration, it is exposed to infection."[1]

So we cultivate joy by clinging to God in times of sorrow and by repenting of all known sin in our lives. Along with these we fix our minds on God and pour ourselves into discovering who he is. The more we know him, the more joyful we will be as the wonders of his character are increasingly revealed to us. Joy is not only a gift but also a responsibility.

---

[1]Elisabeth Elliot, *Discipline: The Glad Surrender* (Grand Rapids, MI: Revell, 1982), 74.

Counterfeit Joy

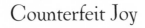

*As for what was sown on rocky ground, this is the one
who hears the word and immediately receives it with joy,
yet he has no root in himself, but endures for a while,
and when tribulation or persecution arises on account of
the word, immediately he falls away.*

M ATTHEW 13:20–21

$\mathcal{U}$ntil this weekend, I hadn't talked to Alex in several years. We used to attend the same church, but life took us in different directions and eventually we fell out of touch. I remember she was a mainstay of the women's Bible study. Her faith was infectious. Under her leadership the study grew quite large. There was just something about Alex that everyone wanted—her joy. Although Alex experienced daily the loneliness of marriage to an unbeliever, she took great delight in sharing her hope in Christ with all around her.

That's why, when I heard from her the other day, I couldn't recognize this Alex as the one I'd known years before. In the intervening years her husband, unable to accept her faith in Christ, had chosen to end the marriage. Alex was now living with another man, also not a believer, and was no longer walking with the Lord. Apparently, for Alex, the cost of following Christ had proven just too high to pay.

Joyful feelings aren't a measure of our Christian commitment. In Alex's case, the joy was real; God had freed her from her sin and the barrenness of life apart from Christ. However, much of her joy sprang from a hope that God would bring her husband to Christ too. When he didn't, her hope died, and so did her joy. The joy promised in Scripture is different from the joy of personal expectation, our hope of some good thing we want God to do in our lives. While it is natural to hope for a good outcome in our difficulties and to trust God for it, we set ourselves up for a spiritual crisis if we expect that things will work out as we think they should.

Joyful feelings are also not a yardstick to be used to determine how well we are doing spiritually. Feelings of closeness to the Lord are a wonderful blessing, but they are not an indicator of God's acceptance of us. Christ is the only indicator. If we blur the distinction, we are going to worry about our spiritual standing whenever the good feelings aren't present.

Joy is indeed a great blessing, but only if it is rightly understood through the lens of Scripture.

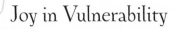

Joy in Vulnerability

So if there is any encouragement in Christ, any comfort
from love, any participation in the Spirit, any affection
and sympathy, complete my joy by being of the same mind,
having the same love, being in full accord and of one mind.

PHILIPPIANS 2 : 1 – 2

*J*oy is the fruit of love given and love received. That's why, if we try to go it alone, we are likely to wind up joyless. Independence and autonomy are American achievements, not biblical ones. However, the desire for independence is the default of our flesh. We all want to be autonomous to one degree or another.

It may be there in the woman who turns down an invitation to dine with friends because she prefers a different restaurant.

It may be there in the woman who prefers to church hop rather than commit to a particular fellowship.

It may be there in the woman who always listens to others' troubles but never shares her own.

We call it independence. A more apt term is self-protection. The Bible calls it selfishness. We cherish our ways, we insist on our rights, and we don't want to get hurt. But love— real love—is never safe. That's because the very nature of love exposes us, leaving us vulnerable to betrayal and rejection. Jesus understood this better than anyone. He spent his life on earth offering love—his very self—only to be rejected by the majority. They wanted him for his miracles, not for himself. He was "a man of sorrows, acquainted with grief," yet he never stopped loving.

God designed us to live alongside one another in love. The Christian family—believers worldwide and in our local fellowship—is God's provision for our comfort, encouragement, affection, and sympathy. When we take the risk not only to give but also to receive comfort, encouragement, affection, and sympathy, the joy that results, despite the inevitable hurts along the way, exposes how utterly joyless and barren a self-protective existence really is.

We are afraid of what will happen if we reveal ourselves, even to (perhaps most especially to) other believers. If others see our sin, if they see us for who we really are, they won't want us. They won't include us. They won't respect us. We all crave love and respect, but living to get them always leads us away from them. If we open up and be real, others will feel free to do so. There is nothing more hollow and Spirit-quenching than a roomful of believers who whitewash their conversation with superficial piety. Real love opens up, and it always leads to joy.

Joy in Knowing Jesus

When they saw the star,
they rejoiced exceedingly with great joy.

MATTHEW 2:10

The wise men rejoiced when they saw the star heralding the birth of Jesus. Why? It is unlikely that they understood at the time all it signified. But they were filled with joy and followed the course of the star as it took them to the Savior incarnate.

The wise men saw the star and rejoiced, but we have seen the life, death, and resurrection of Jesus, which provide us a much fuller picture of the cause of rejoicing. Do we rejoice exceedingly with great joy? So often we receive the good news gladly and gratefully but simply go on about our business. If we know the meaning of the star and all it foreshadowed for us, why aren't we rejoicing with exceeding great joy every moment of our lives? If we really understood it, we would. But, as Todd Augustine said, so often we are in the room with Jesus but we keep him on the other side.[1]

We won't rejoice with exceeding joy until we fully understand who Jesus is, and we won't understand who he is until we recognize the depth of our sin, and we won't grasp the

[1] I am grateful to Todd Augustine for some of the thoughts expressed in this devotion. Todd Augustine, sermon, "Faith and Repentance," August 2, 2009, College Church, Wheaton, IL.

depth of our sin if we keep Jesus on the other side of the room. Is Jesus real to us, or is our understanding of him confined to what he accomplished two thousand years ago? Our love for him is the test. Jesus said, "He who is forgiven little loves little" (Luke 7:47). If we really understood the depth of our sin and how much we have been forgiven, gratitude for Jesus would overwhelm our hearts, and we would love him. If we are keeping him on the other side of the room, it is because we have missed this or are avoiding it.

Is there some sin in your life, either from the past or the present, that you have not brought to the cross? If Jesus doesn't seem real to you, if your heart doesn't genuinely love him as Savior, then you need to consider the possibility and deal honestly with what you uncover. The only remedy—the only way to know the joy of the wise men—is to get real with Christ. Expose your heart to him. Bring him your sin in faith, trusting that he delights to forgive and transform you so that you can truly enjoy him.

Joy in Abiding

*These things I have spoken to you,
that my joy may be in you, and that your joy may be full.*

JOHN 15:11

"These things"—here in John's Gospel Jesus has been giving conditions for joy. This portion of the Gospel is part of what we call the Upper Room Discourse, a special talk Jesus gave to his disciples just before his death. How interesting that he was able to talk about his joy, knowing that the cross lay just ahead.

Jesus has just given the primary condition for joy, and that condition is abiding—abiding in his love and abiding in obedience. He uses everyday imagery, that of a garden, to enable us to understand what it means to abide in him. Jesus Christ is a vine, we are the branches attached to it, and God the Father is the gardener (v. 1). Jesus mentions the pruning process that is necessary to keep plants healthy and flourishing beautifully. He lets us know that God, our Father-Gardener, is going to cut away from the plant any portions that hinder its growth. That means he is going to cut into us in order that our attachment to the primary vine will be stronger and that we will take on more of the characteristics of the vine itself. We are told to abide while this happens, which means that we sit still for the pruning process and allow God to cut what needs to be cut, painful as the cutting might be.

To abide in Christ is to cling to him, and only as we do so will good be produced in us and in our lives. We will find that what we become in the process makes us joyful. Jesus said, "Whoever abides in me and I in him, he it is that bears much fruit, for apart from me you can do nothing" (v. 5). The results of failing to abide couldn't be stated more clearly.

Abiding bring us in tune with God's will, which always brings joy. As we abide in Christ, even our desires are conformed to reflect his so that we find ourselves wanting what he wants. That's what Jesus meant when he said, "If you abide in me, and my words abide in you, ask whatever you wish, and it will be done for you" (v. 8). Abiding shapes our desires, which in turn shape our prayers. If we have found prayer frustrating or seeming to lack answers from God, a failure to abide might be the reason. We simply aren't aligned with God in terms of what we are praying for. Abiding prayer always produces good fruit.

Finally, we abide by obedience. We cannot see the love of God if we choose to live in some sin. Cherishing a pet sin or habit we know is displeasing to God blocks his kindly face from view. "If you keep my commandments, you will abide in my love, just as I have kept my Father's commandments and abide in his love."

Joy and abiding in Christ are inseparable.

Joy in Eating and Drinking

For the kingdom of God is not a matter of eating and drinking but of righteousness and peace and joy in the Holy Spirit.

ROMANS 14:17

*M*ajoring in the minors is what Paul is getting at here in Romans 14:17. He is talking about Christian freedom. Some of us have convictions about things such as drinking alcohol and viewing movies for which the letter rating falls somewhere in the alphabet past G. Others do not. Who is right? It doesn't matter who's right. That is Paul's whole point. What matters is whether everything we do is done for God's glory and for the sake of building up one another in faith. We are not really free to enjoy certain things in the presence of others if doing so discourages their faith, and sometimes the best thing to do is forego the freedom altogether.

What begins as a freedom becomes a prison if we insist on our right to have it. Paradoxically, if we give up a certain liberty for the sake of another's faith, we will find even greater freedom, and accompanying joy as well. "Do not, for the sake of food, destroy the work of God. Everything is indeed clean, but it is wrong for anyone to make another stumble by what he eats. It is good not to eat meat or drink wine or do anything that causes your brother to stumble," Paul writes (vv. 20–21).

Whether to drink alcohol is a much-debated issue among Christians. Many have wine with dinner, and equally as many do not. For those who do, imbibing within biblical parameters entails being careful about when and in front of whom they drink. If our conscience is clear to enjoy that glass of merlot, God takes pleasure in our pleasure, but if we flaunt our enjoyment in the face of someone who believes drinking is wrong, we grieve God and our freedom and joy go out the window. On the other hand, if we believe drinking alcohol is wrong, we are not free to condemn those who believe differently. God is just as grieved when we attempt to forbid something he hasn't expressly forbidden.

From an individual standpoint, freedom and joy will accompany what we eat or drink only when our conscience is clear about it. We do well to suspect ourselves anytime we find the need to tell others (and ourselves) about how very free we are to participate in or partake of a certain something. The old adage about protesting too much contains a lot of truth. True freedom in matters of eating and drinking will typically be accompanied by indifference. Can you take or leave that glass of wine? Then enjoy it, so long as others aren't harmed because you do. We can so easily kid ourselves here. Joyful women are those who recognize the link Scripture makes between eating and drinking—or not—and live accordingly.

The Joy of Wonder

*May the God of hope fill you with all joy and peace
in believing, so that by the power of the Holy Spirit
you may abound in hope.*

ROMANS 15:13

*D*espite the expense and intricate coordination that that
many of us associate with the Christmas season, it remains
a favorite holiday. Some never lose that sense of expectation
and wonder that began with childhood Christmases: lights
twinkling on frosty neighborhood lawns as carolers strolled
the streets, the scent and beauty of the living room Christmas
tree, the aroma of festive food coming from the kitchen,
and heaps of presents under the tree on Christmas morning.
December was a magical month for those of us so blessed
in childhood. For others, however, Christmas was anything
but wonderful. Anyone in law enforcement will tell you that
reports of domestic violence are greatest during the holidays.

Whatever your childhood Christmases were like, you
might have noticed that there's just something about
Christmastime, a certain wonder, which, even when marred
by sin, reflects something of the wonder known by the shep-
herds and the wisemen who saw the star of Bethlehem. The
long-awaited coming of Christ is what underlies the won-

der, the expectation, that something long hoped for is near. Despite the commercialization of Christmas and its overall worldly cast, God still infuses that wonder into the season.

If you recall the sense of joyful expectation from childhood Christmas, then you have tasted something of what God wants for his people all the time in every season. God wills that we live in constant expectation of his appearing. We are to look for him in his Word, in his providences in our daily lives, in our sorrows, in our needs, and in our failures. He comes to us in Christ in all these things, but we miss him because we aren't looking for him, just as we miss the "real meaning" of Christmas when we're caught up in entertaining and gift-giving.

Are we characterized by the wonder of what Christ has done? If not, perhaps it's because we are busy trying to solve our problems in our own way on our own terms. Why look for what God will do if we can simply figure out how to do it ourselves? Self-sufficiency in the Christian life will never bring joy, and it checks hope at the door. We have little wonder because much of the time we don't really want a savior; we want autonomy, self-sufficiency, and for life to work as we think it should. But the promise is that the God of hope will fill us with joy and peace *in believing*, not in getting it all figured out ourselves.

Do you recall the joyful expectation of Christmas past? Do you realize you can live with it every day of the year once you are in Christ? Recapturing the memory of childhood Christmas wonder begins, in a sense, by going back there. "Truly, I say to you, unless you turn and become like children, you will never enter the kingdom of heaven." (Matt. 18:3).

The Fruit of Joy

The fruit of the Spirit is love, joy, peace, patience, kindness,
goodness, faithfulness, gentleness, self-control;
against such things there is no law.
And those who belong to Christ Jesus have crucified
the flesh with its passions and desires.

GALATIANS 5:22–24

Love, joy, peace—who among us doesn't want these traits, this fruit of the Spirit? We set out to cultivate kindness, gentleness, and all the rest, but not too far along in the process, we realize that doing so is easier said than done. In fact, it's impossible. Oh, we might find ourselves a bit more patient with others or more readily able to live out self-control at the dessert buffet, but for the most part, we find that acquiring the traits on Paul's list eludes us.

The reason for that is our misunderstanding of what Paul means by "fruit of the Spirit." Certainly we are called to pursue love and kindness and everything else on the list, but here, in this passage in Galatians, Paul was not giving us a list of traits to cultivate. He was talking about what happens to us as we mature in the Christian life. As we crucify all that belongs to our sinful nature, we are characterized more by Christ than by the passion and desires that governed us before we knew him. As this process takes place, the fruit of the Spirit is manifested in us. The Holy Spirit doesn't give us more love or more faithfulness or more joy. He gives us Christ, and as he does, joy and all the rest are produced within us as the fruit of that union.

Joyful women, therefore, are those that get themselves out of the way and give free rein to Christ. The more of us he has, the more joyful we will be. Our prayers for joy will ring hollow when what we are really seeking is a good, radiant feeling. True joy—fruit of the Spirit joy—comes as we pray to know Christ, and to be made more and more like him. Don Matzat writes:

> Our "religious" focus is not to be directed at spiritual gifts and blessings but at the person of Jesus Christ. If we desire the forgiveness of sins and a righteousness that is acceptable to God, *God gives us Jesus*. If we seek peace, joy, and love, *God gives us Jesus*. If we desire comfort in the midst of sorrow, hope when things look hopeless, assurance when plagued by doubt, and contentment through the changing scenes of life, *God gives us Jesus*. All spiritual gifts are simply manifestations of the new life of Christ dwelling with us, manifested spontaneously as we walk in the Spirit by directing our consciousness unto Jesus.[1]

---

[1]Don Matzat, *Christ Esteem: Where the Search for Self-Esteem Ends* (Eugene, OR: Harvest House, 1990), 109; emphasis in original.

Joy in All God's Gifts

As for the rich in this present age, charge them not to be haughty, nor to set their hopes on the uncertainty of riches, but on God, who richly provides us with everything to enjoy.

1 TIMOTHY 6:17

*W*hat started as an economic downturn in 2008 quickly spiraled into an outright crisis. An expert in the financial industry told me that signs of the crisis had been evident for years, but they were ignored by the majority. When the crisis finally hit, the finger-pointing began. Citizens blamed the government, the government blamed Wall Street, Wall Street blamed society-wide individual debt, and the media blamed everybody. But the overlooked reality is that such crises are inevitable in a culture of greed. Those who "set their hearts" on riches are greedy, a condition that describes all of us to some extent.

The problem is, as Paul points out, riches are uncertain. The economic crisis is proof of that. When the crisis first hit and its impact was not yet known, we believers were handed a unique opportunity to demonstrate to a watching world that life is so much more than secure retirement accounts. Did we demonstrate that? Hopefully many of us did; however, just as many panicked right along with our non-Christian neighbors. Whatever our response, Paul says, it was conditioned upon where our hearts were set.

Are our hearts set on God or on our bank accounts? Our response to situations like the financial crisis reveals the answer. A heart set on God recognizes a joy-producing truth: he delights to give us things to enjoy. God is a giver. His character is one of generosity so that when he gives, he gives lavishly. When our hearts are set on something as uncertain as a nice fat IRA, we lose sight of just how richly God has blessed us. Do we stop to consider how many gifts are handed to us on something like a simple evening walk? The ability to move our legs and walk is a tremendous gift. Sight to see the landscape and the sunset is another, as are the intricate flowers we encounter along the way that smell so good. The heart-warming sense of belonging that comes through the friendly greeting from the neighbor across the street is still another. If we consider the fact that every aspect of an evening walk is a gift from God, how much more, then, must we see our homes, husbands, friendships, health, and jobs?

In a fallen world, none of these things is perfect, but the Giver of them has perfectly ordered them just for us. In that sense each aspect of our lives, including the imperfect or downright trying ones, is just as it is supposed to be. If our hearts are set on God, we not only see the truth of this in all we have but we can't help but rejoice that we are so blessed by our generous heavenly Father.

Joy in Hard Things

Count it all joy, my brothers,
when you meet trials of various kinds.

JAMES 1:2

A good friend quoted this verse to me recently for the usual reason it gets quoted: absence of joy in the midst of a trial. I had no joy in the trial I was undergoing at the time. In fact, I was stuck in misery. My friend reminded me of God's sovereignty over the circumstances, but the reminder did little to relieve my anguish and restore me to joy because I was so focused on the situation that I couldn't see it through a biblical lens. Looking at our problems rather then at God and his Word always distorts our view of reality.

God cares more about our joy than we often do, which is why he doesn't leave us alone in our misery. He seeks to get us into a corner so that we will see clearly once again and realize that our difficulties are all under his control. God orchestrates for us and in us the humility we need in order to see that God is a kind Father and compassionate friend who brings hard situations into our lives so that he can show us our need for grace and deepen our relationship with him. Such humility is necessary in order to "count it all joy."

The joy of trials is rarely found in the circumstances of

our difficulties. Rather, it is found when we stop fighting against what God is doing and seek his purposes and priorities, which always without exception are designed for our welfare. Whatever the difficulty—even one brought about by our sin—we can leave the outcome in God's hands. We don't have to hover over every detail in a desperate attempt to solve the problem. When no biblical solution lies before us, we simply cling to God in the midst of our pain and trust him to handle it for us in the way he chooses. If we do so, before long his kindness, power, and good purposes (some of them, at least) will be evident to us. Joy will return, even if our circumstances don't change. Counting our trials all joy, as James instructed, is much more than mentally agreeing that God knows best. It is humbling our hearts to the pain he allows, trusting that his love and providence underlie every detail of the situation.

Joy in Today

This is the day that the LORD has made;
let us rejoice and be glad in it.

PSALM 118:24

Today is the day for joy, not tomorrow or the day after that or next week. Too often our joy is based on what we hope tomorrow will bring because we don't like what today holds. Oh, there may be nothing terribly wrong with today, but the humdrum routine is wearing, and we are convinced that the next thing on the horizon might spice things up a bit.

For some of us, however, the hundrum routine is the least of our concerns. Something in our life is terribly wrong. We are facing a crisis or a loss, and we see no cause for rejoicing in what today holds.

Maybe for others getting through yet one more day with seemingly unanswered prayer seems impossible—the single woman heading out the door to a job she doesn't really care about because she has no family to stay home and care for, or the would-be mother receiving news of yet another friend's pregnancy.

Whether today holds humdrum routine or painful crisis or something in between, it is exactly as it's supposed to be because God has so ordered it. "The God who made the

world and everything in it, being Lord of heaven and earth
. . . made from one man every nation of mankind to live on
all the face of the earth, having determined allotted periods
and the boundaries of their dwelling place," Paul said (Acts
17:24–26). And the psalmist praises God, saying:

> *Your eyes saw my unformed substance;*
> *in your book were written, every one of them,*
> *the days that were formed for me,*
> *when as yet there was none of them.* (Ps. 139:16)

Where we live, our marital status, the family we have, our
bank account—even the weather outside our window—are
kept under the sovereign scrutiny and ordering of our heavenly
Father and friend. Even the hairs of our head are numbered
(Matt. 10:30).

What does this mean? It means that if we cannot—will
not—rejoice in today, we are rejecting God's providence. It
means that we believe we have better ideas for today than
God's plan. It means we don't trust. It means we are rebels.
Since everything about our today is "ordered in all things and
secure" (2 Sam. 23:5) by our kind, generous, loving God,
then no matter what it holds we have cause for rejoicing, even
in the most painful circumstances.

Think, too, of all the blessings right in front of us.
Someone I know made a conscious effort to do just that, and
by the time she arrived at work, her mood had turned from
gloom to joy. She thanked God for the clock radio that awakened her with a favorite song. She thanked him for her closet
full of clothes as she selected an outfit and for the smell of
coffee brewing in the kitchen while she dressed. She thanked
him for the thirty minutes of quiet privacy to read her Bible

and pray while a pair of cardinals twittered outside the window. She thanked him for the fact that she could walk to the bus and for the empty seat awaiting her as she boarded it. She thanked God for the cloud cover that would make working indoors on a summer day just a bit more palatable. When she arrived at work, she thanked God for her colleagues and for the work on her desk and for steady employment. What would otherwise have been a humdrum day became a day of rejoicing by 9 AM.

If we want joy today—just as it is—we need only remember that this is the day the Lord has made and then choose to rejoice and be glad in it.

Joy in God's Providences

Rejoice always, pray without ceasing,
give thanks in all circumstances;
for this is the will of God in Christ Jesus for you.

1 THESSALONIANS 5:16-18

*W*e have an endless fascination with books and sermons on how to know God's will for our lives, but sometimes what underlies this passionate interest is not so much a desire to please God as it is a desire to please ourselves. We want a blueprint for happiness, and we know God has the power to provide it. But God's primary will for us is not circumstantial happiness, which is why our attempts to harness him for that purpose never quite work. Until we taste the sort of happiness God desires for us, we are going to latch on to every new book or blog post or sermon about guidance, hoping that this one will provide the right formula.

Scripture is our blueprint for guidance, for knowing the will of God, and it gives us all we need to map out our lives. We miss this, however, when we are looking for steps, not principles. The Bible provides us with guidance principles—what pleases God and what does not, what is wise and what is foolish. It is by following these principles that we live out God's will in our individual lives.

Paul tells us three things that are God's will for each of us: "Rejoice always, pray without ceasing, give thanks in all circumstances; for this is the will of God in Christ Jesus for you" (1 Thess. 5:16–18). We have there joy, gratitude, and constant prayer in every circumstance. They are always linked. Joy springs from gratitude and prayer.

The opposite is also true: pessimism and grumbling are linked to depression. It is perverse, then, that we so readily feel such sinful negativity. We choose to take a glass-half-empty outlook and complain about our lives, and the price we pay is our joy and peace. It just makes no sense. Rejoicing and giving thanks are how we say, "Not my will, God, but yours be done." Rejoicing and giving thanks are the essence of humility, and it is the way God connects our hearts to his good purposes in all things, big and small. That is God's will, and if we follow it, we will be characterized by joy, and we will much more easily discern his will for the details of our lives.

Joy from Failure

The Spirit of the Lord GOD is upon me,
because the LORD has anointed me
to bring good news to the poor;
he has sent me to bind up the brokenhearted,
to proclaim liberty to the captives,
and the opening of the prison to those who are bound;
to proclaim the year of the LORD's favor,
and the day of vengeance of our God;
to comfort all who mourn;
to grant to those who mourn in Zion—
to give them a beautiful headdress instead of ashes,
the oil of gladness instead of mourning,
the garment of praise instead of a faint spirit;
that they may be called oaks of righteousness,
the planting of the LORD, that he may be glorified.

ISAIAH 61:1–3

The riches of the Messiah promised by Isaiah have all come true. In Christ we get healing for our broken hearts, freedom from the sin that holds us in bondage, comfort in our sorrows, beauty for ashes, joy in place of mourning, praise more potent than fear, and the strength of righteousness.

The trouble is that in order to understand and know the comfort, freedom, and beauty, we first have to know the broken heart, the bondage, the sorrow, and the ashes. Since that is true, our lives here on earth contain a good bit of the painful side of things. What a blessing, then, that joy isn't restricted to the times of comfort and strength! Sometimes, in fact, it is most keenly felt in sorrow and weakness, and that is sure to be the case when we cling to God in our pain rather than fight in our strength to get out of it.

We all have ashes in our lives left from the wreckage of our sin and the sins of others, but out of that very wreckage Jesus builds something beautiful. He did it with Mary Magdalene and with Peter and with the woman at the well in Samaria. He does it with you and me. From out of our failures he builds something new and glorious—a beautiful headdress—that wouldn't have come about any other way. The failures that mar our lives are never the end of the story. J. I. Packer writes:

> God can and does restore the years that the locusts have eaten (see Joel 2:25). Scripture shows us a number of saints making great and grievous mistakes about the will of God for them—Jacob fooling his father, Moses murdering the Egyptian, David numbering the people, Peter boycotting Gentile believers—yet none became incurably second class. On the contrary, they were each forgiven and restored. This is how all true saints live.[1]

Regret is a tragic waste. Why linger in it when such beauty is held out to us? Finding joy in our failures begins by looking to Jesus and asking God to redeem our ashes by creating beauty from them. Let's look for it. Let's hope for it with joyful expectation.

---

[1] J. I. Packer, *God's Plan for You* (Wheaton, IL: Crossway, 2001), 91.

Joy in God's Care

He has made everything beautiful in its time.

ECCLESIASTES 3:11

*P*eople mean well, but offering random speculation about the particulars of what God is doing in difficult situations is largely unhelpful and often (if not always) inaccurate. "This has been miserable for you, but perhaps God did it for the benefit of so-and-so." There is little comfort in such remarks because they imply that God sacrifices the well-being of one for that of another. There is also little truth in such remarks because God is much bigger than what such comments imply.

First, he is bigger in how he loves. "The LORD is good to all, and his mercy is over all that he has made" (Ps. 145:9). God's kindness and mercy overshadow every individual in every circumstance at every point in time and in our lives. Second, our all-knowing and all-powerful God is bigger in how he oversees the details of every molecule and event and life. "The lot is cast into the lap, but its every decesion is from the Lord" (Prov. 16:33).

Because God is that big, we know our suffering is never solely for the benefit of someone else at our expense. It is equally for our benefit. God's purposes is all human suffering are beyond our ability to fathom, but whoever suffers and however the situation plays out, it is always so that God's glory may be shown more fully to all involved—somehow, some way. We don't always see it immediately, however, and sometimes we never do, but we can believe it's true. The Word tells us that God makes everything beautiful in the time that he has determined to show the beauty. Knowing this, we can rejoice no matter what befalls us and those we love. Philip Ryken writes:

> Something "beautiful" is something good; it is right, pleasing, and appropriate. It is in this sense that God can be said to have beautiful timing. At whatever time he does things, God is always right on time. He knows when it is time for breaking down and building up, for keeping and casting away, for war and for peace. When the Preacher says that God "has made everything beautiful in its time" (Eccles. 3:11), he is not just talking about the way that God made the world in the first place, but about the way that he has ruled it ever since. The seasons of nature and the patterns of human activity are under his sovereign superintendence and providential care. From beginning to end, God does everything decently and in order.[1]

This is why joy is possible, no matter what.

---

[1]Philip G. Ryken, *Ecclesiastes*, Preaching the Word Commentary Series (Wheaton, IL: Crossway, 2010), n.p.

Joy in Prayer

Pray without ceasing.

1 THESSALONIANS 5:17

*D*o you struggle with prayer? Perhaps you worry about doing it incorrectly. Maybe you wonder whether you pray for the wrong things. Perhaps you are anxious about where confession fits in. Must you be sure to confess every sin you can think of before asking God for anything? Perhaps you have no trouble praying about the big crises in life—a rebellious teenager, cancer, unemployment—but when it comes to the lesser concerns—hormone-based mood swings, a visit from your in-laws, exclusion from a social gathering—you hesitate to pray, fearing that God will take no notice. You are worried about bothering him with trivialities. Can you relate to these concerns? If so, you are not alone. Many of us hold misconceptions about prayer, and God delights to clear away the clouds so we may enter in with joy.

Joy in prayer begins with recognizing that God cares about every detail of our lives. He cares enough to number every hair on our heads (Matt. 10:30); therefore, nothing is too trivial to take to him in prayer. Jesus instructed his followers to approach God as a child comes to a father—with uncomplicated words and confidence of being heard and helped.

Prayer is an amazing gift. It is the God-ordained vehicle for communicating with him. Prayer is the place where we tell God how awesome he is and the way to thank him for all he has done for us and all he continues to do. Prayer is also the means for telling God our concerns about well, everything. There is nothing off-limits, and God never grows weary of hearing from us. In his first letter to the Thessalonians, Paul wrote that we should "pray without ceasing" (1 Thess. 5:17). In prayer we can talk to God about the same things we discuss with the people who are closest to us, and even more so. God does not want us to fret over our lives. Instead, as Paul instructs the Philippians, "Do not be anxious about anything, but in everything by prayer and supplication with thanksgiving let your requests be made known to God" (4:6). Do you have a family problem? How about concerns with finances, or health, or friendships, or your purpose in life? God cares about all these things. Absolutely nothing falls outside the scope of his loving attention.

Not only are we invited to tell God about our concerns, but we are also encouraged to ask him for the things we need. Jesus instructed us to pray for our daily bread, and by that he meant more than just food. He was referring to everything we need to live our lives. Although God already knows what we need before we ask, he has designed our provision to come to us through the means of prayer. The Bible tells us: "This is the confidence that we have towards him, that if we ask anything according to his will, he hears us. And if we know that he hears us in whatever we ask, we know that we have the requests we have asked of him" (1 John 5:14–15). If we ask anything according to God's will, we can be confident of receiving those things.

Perhaps, but that is not the sort of thing John had in mind in this passage. John's point is that the prayers of those who live in submission to Christ, seeking to please him in all things, are much more likely to be in line with God's will in the first place. Prayers in which we can be confident of receiving what we ask for look like this:

> "Father, please heal this cancer if doing so will bring glory to you, but if I and others will know more of your love through not healing it, then so be it."

> "God, if I can better serve you married, then bring along a husband. If not, then keep me single."

> "Lord, you know I need an income, and I've been pursuing it in this direction. But perhaps you have another means in mind. Please guide my life to the path you have best marked out for me to live most closely with you and reflect your goodness to others."

The Bible doesn't tell us God's will in such matters, but we can entrust our cares to God, asking simply that his will be done. When we do that, we can bank on the best outcome, whatever it may be.

Prayer will be a joyless task so long as we view it as no more than something on the to-do list of our personal agenda. Prayer that brings us into fellowship with God and into his agenda is joy-filled.

Joy in Discernment

Solid food is for the mature, for those who have their powers of discernment trained by constant practice to distinguish good from evil.

HEBREWS 5:14

*W*hen is a word of rebuke better than a word of comfort? When are we to act on circumstances, and when are we to sit back and wait for God to act? Discernment is the ability to recognize how to apply God's Word accurately to a given situation. The Bible has a lot of black-and-white answers, where right and wrong are clearly distinguished. Yet so much of our daily lives involves gray areas—situations in which the black-and-white answers just don't seem to help us very much, or where the clear answers of Scripture are easily misapplied.

How is a mother to love her teenage daughter who is caught up with a gang of troublemakers? What is the best way to help a friend who is making a life-altering decision that seems unwise, to our way of thinking? Sometimes the most loving thing to do in such situations doesn't seem very loving at first. Is confrontation appropriate or should we simply pray? Do we involve others in the situation or would doing so be a breach of confidence? Even our attempts to love others are tainted by our sin, which is why we need Spirit-guided discernment in order to love others well.

Spiritual discernment enables us to distinguish between good, better, and best, and it enables us to apply God's Word in loving ways to each particular situation we face. The link to love is crucial. The actions that result from Spirit-given discernment will always be accompanied by love. A parent may be able to discern when disciplining a child is necessary, but if the discipline isn't tempered with mercy it will be administered in anger rather than love. Discernment without love will not result in godly action; discernment without love cannot properly be called discernment at all, at least not in the biblical sense. As Paul wrote elsewhere: "If I have prophetic powers, and understand all mysteries and all knowledge, and if I have all faith, so as to remove mountains, but have not love, I am nothing" (1 Cor. 13:2).

Discernment linked with love results in what's best for everyone involved and brings the most glory to God. This discernment carries joy in its wake.

Joy in Trust

Rejoice in the Lord always; again I will say, Rejoice.
Let your reasonableness be known to everyone.
The Lord is at hand; do not be anxious about anything,
but in everything by prayer and supplication with
thanksgiving let your requests be made known to God.
And the peace of God, which surpasses all understanding,
will guard your hearts and your minds in Christ Jesus.

PHILIPPIANS 4:4–7

*I*f we give free rein to worrisome thoughts, anxiety is going to become a habit to which we find ourselves enslaved. Perhaps you know exactly what I mean. If so, think about this: since God's will for us is joy, we can trust that it is his will for us to be free from anxiety.

The biblical antidote to anxiety is prayer. Paul says, "Rejoice always," which we can do because "the Lord is at hand." He is present everywhere and in everything. There is nothing about us or our lives that is not governed by his love, his power, and his goodness. Paul writes that our reasonableness, or gentleness, should be evident to others.

Reasonableness—what does Paul mean? He is saying that trusting God is reasonable because God is totally in charge, all loving, and all good. Doubt and anxiety are, therefore, *un*reasonable.

Although we may feel that refraining from anxiety is impossible sometimes, refraining is indeed possible since the Bible never tells us to do something that God has not equipped us to do. The equipping is presented here in Philippians as prayer, taking our concerns straight to God rather than fretting over them. Nothing is off limits. Prayer is to be offered "in all things," Paul says, which means there is nothing we can't take to God. Sometimes we think we shouldn't bother God with the little things of life, but Paul says "all things." Jesus himself said that God has numbered the hairs on our heads—something we don't even take time to do—so if God bothers himself about this, he is certainly interested in all the things about daily life that cause us concern. Are you worried about a relationship? Your weight? Intimacy with your spouse? Whatever it may be, God welcomes our prayers.

Paul also tells us how to go about making use of this antidote to anxiety—with supplication and thanksgiving. We are to tell God our concerns, hopes, desires, and needs, and then thank him that he will provide in the best possible way. This is why we have great reason to trust and no reason for anxiety. If it were up to us to determine what's best for our own lives and the lives of those we love, we'd have good reason for anxiety. Only God sees everything—past, present, and future. "My thoughts are not your thoughts, neither are your ways my ways, declares the LORD. For as the heavens are higher than the earth, so are my ways higher than your ways and my thoughts than your thoughts" (Isa. 55:6–9).

It is God's will that we be free of anxiety. Isn't this great reason for rejoicing? He wants us to discover that he can take good care of us. He wants us to trust that he is in charge, even when the way looks dark and we cannot see evidences of his goodness. God is good to us each and every moment. Worry, anxiety, and stress rob us of joy, but trusting God produces it. Paul knew this. Paul believed this. Therefore, he couldn't help but rejoice. If we are in Christ, the same privilege—the same joy—belongs to us too.

Joy in Full Provision

My God shall supply all your needs according to his riches in glory in Christ Jesus.

PHILIPPIANS 4:19

*I*n his brief note of thanks near the end of his letter to the Philippians, Paul expressed gratitude to his friends at Philippi because they had provided for some of his material needs. He was grateful not so much for the physical comfort but for the loving partnership such gifts prove.

According to Paul, being generous is always possible. We are free to give sacrificially of our money, time, talents—all of our resources—because God provides all we need from a well that never runs dry. Although Paul's statement is made in the context of giving, God's provision for his children applies to every area of life. God promises to supply all our need.

What an amazing promise! God's supply isn't limited to just the spiritual sphere of life; his supply covers everything. That means that there is absolutely nothing we need that God won't amply provide. There is no promise, however, that we will get everything we want, even though God in his goodness fulfills so many of our heart's desires. God is not stingy. Like any good father, he loves to lavish good things on his children; but like any good father, he also knows that some of the things we want wouldn't be good for us.

Do we believe this promise, that God will supply all our needs—our real needs? Perhaps we can recall an occasion where it seemed that God let us down. We didn't get what we wanted and thought we so desperately needed. The truth is that he knows we really don't need many of the things we think we need. We so easily confuse our wants with our needs, and often only our good, wise Father knows the difference between the two. Jesus said, "If you then, who are evil, know how to give good gifts to your children, how much more will your Father who is in heaven give good things to those who ask him!" (Matt. 7:11).

We can trust that God always gives what is best for us and will surely provide for our needs. The measure of this supply, says Paul, is "according to the riches in glory in Christ Jesus." What does this mean? Here is how James Boice preached it: "Do not think you can ever exhaust the riches of God by your needs, however great they may be. Can the finite exhaust the infinite? Can that which is corrupt exhaust that which is incorruptible? Can the part exhaust the whole? Can man exhaust God? It is impossible."

If we really believed that each and every one of our needs is supplied to us in Christ, we would overflow with joy.

Joy from Rejoicing

Rejoice in the Lord always; again I will say, Rejoice.

PHILIPPIANS 4:4

*D*espite the prison guard hovering over him, Paul was characterized by joy as he wrote to his friends at Philippi. In the first portion of the letter, Paul writes that he prays for them with joy. He is filled with rejoicing because Christ is being proclaimed (1:18). Paul will continue to rejoice, he says, because he trusts he will sooner or later be delivered from his troubles (1:18–19). Paul wants the Philippians to experience joy in their faith (1:25). Then Paul really warms up in chapter 2, where he expresses joy in the unity of believers (v. 2). We are amazed to see that Paul rejoices even at the thought of sacrificing his life for Christ (v. 17). Paul urges the Philippians to rejoice with him (v. 18), and to rejoice at the coming of his co-laborer Epaphroditus (vv. 28–29). Paul intensifies the importance of joy in chapter 3, where in the opening verse he issues a command to rejoice. As he prepares to close his letter, we discover his joy in the shared partnership of the Philippians (4:1), as well as an imperative push for joy: "Rejoice in the Lord always; again I will say, Rejoice" (4:4).

Paul is in prison, yet his dominant mood is joy. What

mood defines *us* today? Are we buried under a weight of stress as we think about our responsibilities at home or at work, or about family concerns? Perhaps right now we find ourselves alone in the world, either because we are single or widowed, or because we have been tragically abandoned by someone we loved and trusted. Some of us lack joy because we want something or someone so badly that our desire has hijacked our heart, and we have become so obsessed with obtaining what we want—and so desperately think we need—that we have become incapable of joy. Whatever our circumstances, are we characterized by joy or are we fearful and depressed?

Joy just seems impossible sometimes. So how was Paul able to experience joy while bound in chains? He was able because his joy was not dependent on his circumstances. Paul's joy stemmed from the fact that his entire life, his every goal, and all his thoughts were centered on Jesus Christ. For him, it was simply a matter of focus.

"I can't feel joyful right now," we sometimes say, but Paul's words concerning joy and rejoicing weren't written as helpful suggestions; they were imperatives. In other words, joy is obedience. How can that be? How can we help what we feel? We just can't muster up joyful feelings; that's true. But we can rejoice, which sooner or later leads to joyful feelings. Rejoicing is not a feeling. It is joy in action. It is the humble willingness to offer God praise and thanks in all things, regardless of how we feel at the moment. Are we willing?

Joy in Christ Alone

If anyone else thinks he has reason for confidence in the flesh,
I have more.

PHILIPPIANS 3:4

*P*aul certainly had a lot going for himself before becoming a Christian, but once Christ found him, Paul let go of his personal assets.

Let's think about this from a personal standpoint. What are we tempted to rest on? Where does our confidence lie? It cannot lie in the fact that we go to a good church and have our doctrinal T's crossed. That is a help, but it can never be our spiritual security. Nor can our security rest on our Bible reading or our service in the church nursery or our donations to the homeless shelter. Our confidence also cannot rest on the strong faith of our husband, the good behavior of our children, or the fact that we were raised in a Christian home. None of that is an indicator of our security in Christ. It is Christ—and Christ alone—who saves us. Charles Spurgeon wrote, "Ah, what a mercy it is that it is not your hold of Christ that saves you, but his hold of you! What a sweet fact that it is not how you grasp his hand, but his grasp of yours that saves you."

We cannot "do" our relationship with God by ourselves.

We call God "Father," seek our provision from him, and enjoy our relationship with him, but it is never just God the Father and us. Christ is always in the middle of that relationship. We call God "Father" only through Jesus Christ. It is our union with him that enables our relationship with God, rather than anything in or about ourselves.

So, where does our confidence lie? How do we know we are safe and secure? How do we know for sure that God loves us? If we look within ourselves we will find no security, because there is nothing in us that is sufficient for establishing and maintaining a relationship with God.

We are prone to view our daily lives as a measure of God's favor, of how well we are doing with him. If things are going well, we reason that God must be pleased. If our circumstances are difficult, we assume that somehow we have fallen out of God's favor. He does discipline us when we sin, and he sifts out hidden sins through trials and testing, but if we are his in Christ, the sifting is an indicator that we are safely within the boundary of his favor.

If we look at what is going on in our lives as a barometer for our standing with God, we will find ourselves open and vulnerable to fear and doubt. Sooner or later, something is going to pull the rug out from under our lives, and if we have looked to our circumstances for assurance of our right standing with God, where will we be then?

Christ is the only foundation for our confidence, but because of that, we have every reason for joy. We are inadequate; our circumstances are unstable. Christ alone is unchanging, and therefore he is the only basis for our security. But what security it is!

Joy in Submission

Humble yourselves, therefore, under the mighty hand
of God so that at the proper time he may exalt you,
casting all your anxieties on him, because he cares for you.

1 PETER 5:6-7

Relinquishing self-reliance is the path to joy, even when the path is at times crooked and hard going. Letting go and learning to depend on Christ alone for everything is the hardest thing we will ever do, since self-reliance is our default mode. Relinquishment was apparently not an easy process for Paul, either: "I have suffered the loss of all things," he wrote (Phil. 3:8). Letting go of self-sufficiency—even for Paul—entailed suffering. Dying to self-will, even when we trust how much we will gain by doing so, is a painful process. It hurts to let go of self-reliance, self-confidence, and self-sufficiency. Our ingrained pride doesn't want a savior. We want to make life work on our terms. It feels natural to carve out our own way, even though it never works.

When Christ gets hold of our hearts by faith, the Holy Spirit begins the process of conforming us to our Savior, which entails leaving the old self behind. This process, although hard, always leads to joy. If we will trust God and follow him without reservation, we'll discover, as Paul did,

that everything we leave behind is less than nothing compared to what we gain. Paul came to view everything he lost
as worthless compared to the surpassing worth of knowing
Christ Jesus. It is evident that he had no regrets because he
discovered that the gains far exceeded any price he had paid.

Is Paul's goal—Christ alone—our goal? If not, perhaps
that's because we have not tasted how truly freeing and wonderful it is to let go of ourselves and submit to the loving over-
sight of God. Perhaps it is because we have not yet discovered
that our personal confidence and self-sufficiency aren't going
to bring us what we hope they will. What are we waiting for?
It really is true that we have nothing to lose. Only when we
accept that true joy comes through full submission will we
know joy that lasts.

Joy in God's Love

*It is my prayer that your love may abound more and more
with knowledge and all discernment so that you may
approve what is excellent and so be pure and blameless
for the day of Christ, filled with the fruit of righteousness that
comes through Jesus Christ, to the glory and praise of God.*

PHILIPPIANS 1:9–11

There are certain prayers we can be confident that God will answer, and we know this because they are recorded for us in Scripture as examples of how God wants us to pray. God wants us to ask him for the things we find in Bible prayers, and they are the things he is most eager to give us. Paul's prayer in Philippians 1:1–9 has a number of them.

Of what can we be confident of receiving if we pray this prayer? Let's list the blessings: increased love; deeper knowledge of God; the ability to discern good, better, and best; purity; blamelessness; the fruit of righteousness that comes to us through Christ Jesus; and the opportunity to glorify God.

That sounds good and right, we say, but what does it all really mean? We know these are good things to pray for, but because we don't really understand the particular ways these blessings work out in our lives, we are less inclined to pray for them. We are much more driven to pray for our earthly needs and desires because we have a clear handle on the benefits they provide. But, in actuality, the blessings in Paul's prayer are richer and more fulfilling than any earthly blessing could ever be.

Paul prays first for abounding love. Love for whom? Is he talking about love for God or love for one another? We get our answer if we consider Jesus' words about the greatest of all commandments: "You shall love the Lord your God with all your heart and with all your soul and with all your mind. This is the great and first commandment. And a second is like it: You shall love your neighbor as yourself" (Matt. 22:36–39). Based on that commandment, we can take Paul's meaning to be both love for God and love for one another. Paul is praying that we would grow in our love for God, which, in turn, will result in an outpouring of love for others.

The apostle John wrote, "We love because he first loved us" (1 John 4:19), so we see that our love for God and others grows as it parallels our growth in understanding of how much we are loved by him. Isn't that the greatest blessing we can conceive of—knowing we are loved so much that there is nothing we can do to destroy it? As we come to comprehend the depth of God's love for us, we will overflow with joy and love for God and these people he places in our lives.

This, then, is our greatest source of joy—to comprehend God's love for us. It is also the primary need for everyone around us, no matter how pressing their earthly trials and troubles. God wants us to be gripped with the depth of his love—love most clearly seen in the fact that he sent his only Son to die in order to bring us near to him—and when we do, others will see it and come to know their real need also.

Personal Reflections

Personal Reflections

Personal Reflections

Personal Reflections

Personal Reflections

Personal Reflections

Personal Reflections

Personal Reflections